FAITH

365

Bree Abbington

ISBN: 0615982670
ISBN-13: 978-0615982670

DEDICATION

To all of the people in my life who have shown me what
real faith is.

PREFACE

Faith means something different to each individual who ever walked upon this planet. For me, "faith" was defined the evening of August 10, 2012. I had boarded an airplane from Austin to Los Angeles. The plane had taken off a couple hours late, so there were already many annoyed passengers. The airline attendants and gate-workers were doing their best to keep everyone cheerful; however, there were already many people grumbling about the delay.

The take-off was uneventful. Five minutes into the flight we had a "mechanical failure." The result was the plane listed from port to starboard and back at some very alarming angles. The pilot came on to make an announcement, "We have obviously had a mechanical failure. We will be making an emergency landing in Austin in three minutes." I was alone on the flight, so three minutes is a lot of time to actually think.

I closed my eyes and went deep inside. I sent up a prayer, "God, you've got this. Right?"

I opened my eyes and looked around the cabin. I had an aisle seat, so I enjoyed a pretty good view of people, and faces and reactions. It was right then I fully realized what faith is. It is not owned by any one domination or religion. It cuts across socio-economic classes. It is something so much more.

After my prayer, brief as it was, I understood it was or was not my day to die and God had it. God means different things to different people depending on how they were raised, but it is really the same thing – a higher power who has control over the chaos. I had complete peace knowing there was nothing I could do to change this situation. "God's will be done."

I began looking at the faces of the other passengers. It was so evident who had faith and who didn't. The people of faith were able to calmly await further instructions. The people without were doing everything from sobbing to trying to grab their overhead carry-ons contrary to the orders it remain seated. As if any of the things in the carry-on could change what would or would not happen.

A minute out we were given final instructions. The landing itself – totally uneventful. For me, an unanticipated overnight in Austin, Texas. There are far worse fates!

This book is about faith. A few disclaimers are in order. First, in my opinion faith is not monopolized by one religion or one domination. Early on in World Religions class I learned it is the one common thread among all major and most minor beliefs. The quotes you will find here range from major religious leaders of all faiths. Second, faith is not owned by any religion or domination. This why you will find quotes from John Lennon, Garth Brooks and many modern novelists. Third, any quote that does not have a credit is by the savant simply known as "unknown."

FAITH
365

Faith is the strength by which a shattered world
shall emerge into the light.
-Helen Keller, activist

Faith is like Wi-Fi it's invisible, but it has the
power to connect you to what you need.

Faith is to believe what you do not see; the
reward of this faith is to see what you believe.
-Saint Augustine, theologian

When you have come to the edge
of all light that you know and
are about to drop off into the darkness of the
unknown, faith is knowing that
one of two things will happen:
there will be something solid to stand on
or you will be taught to fly.
-Patrick Overton, educator, poet

Ultimately, blind faith is the only kind.
- Mason Cooley, aphorist

Worry looks around.
Regret looks back.
Faith looks forward.

Faith is taking the first step even when you don't
see the whole staircase, just take the first step.
-Martin Luther King, Jr., civil rights leader

Doubt is a pain too lonely to know that faith is
his twin brother.
-Khalil Gibran, writer and artist

Faith is strongest when you are completely
hemmed in on all sides with no escape plan, and
no backup plan.

Faith activates God – Fear activates the enemy.
- Joel Osteen, pastor

Belief is a wise wager.
Granted that faith cannot be proved,
what harm will come to you if you gamble on its
truth and it proves to be false?
If you gain, you gain all;
if you lose, you lose nothing.
Wager, then, without hesitation,
that He exists.
- Blaise Pascal, mathematician

The keys to patience are acceptance and faith.
Accept things as they are,
And look realistically at the world around you.
Have faith in yourself, and
in the direction you have chosen.
- Ralph Martson,
played in the National Football League
with the Boston Bulldogs in 1929.
At the time of publication, age 107

Faith is about believing. You don't know how it will happen, but you know it will.

If patience is worth anything, it must endure to the end of time. And living faith will last in the midst of the blackest storm.
-Mahatma Gandhi, political leader

Where there is hope, there is faith.
Where there is faith, miracles happen.

God will never give you anything you can't handle, so don't stress.
-Kelly Clarkson, country music artist

Forget all the reasons why it won't work and believe the one reason why it will.

Our faith comes in moments; our vice is habitual.
-Ralph Waldo Emerson, poet

Faith is not simply a patience
that passively suffers until the storm is past.
Rather, it is a spirit that bears things –
with resignations, yes,
but above all,
with blazing, serene hope.
-Corazon Aquino, former President of the
Philippians

When we hear someone say "No"
it just means it's not time yet,
each and every "No" is a test of our faith.
Stay strong and hold on a little bit longer.
- Karen Kostyla, counselor

Have a little faith, someone has to. It will all work out, it always does.

God enters by a private door into every individual.
-Ralph Waldo Emerson, poet

You must believe in yourself.

Always believe that something wonderful is about to happen.

We are twice armed if we fight with faith.
-Plato, teacher

Faith is not being sure where you're going, but going anyway

A man lost everything in a fire.
The next day he placed a sign board
in front of his business:
Everything burnt but
luckily faith and confidence undamaged.
Business starts tomorrow.

Listen to the mustn'ts, child.
Listen to the don'ts.
Listen to the shouldn'ts,
the impossibles,
the won'ts.
Listen to the never haves.
Then listen close to me...
Anything can happen, child.
Anything can be.
-Shel Silverstein, writer

Faith is the activity where the human will interacts with the divine will in space and time.

A faith is a necessity to a man. Woe to him who believes in nothing.
-Victor Hugo, writer

Keep your eyes on your faith, because sometimes it's all you'll ever have

Faith ends where worry beings, and worry ends where faith begins.

If fear is cultivated it will become stronger, if faith is cultivated it will achieve mastery.
- John Paul Jones, naval officer

She took the leap and built her wings on the way down.

Magic is
believing in yourself.
If you can do that,
you can make anything happen.
-Johann Wolfgang von Goethe, writer and
politician

I cheated on my fears,
broke up with my doubts,
got engaged to my faith, and
now I'm married to my dreams.

Faith is not belief without proof, but is trust without reservation

Physical strength can never permanently withstand the impact of spiritual force.
-Franklin D. Roosevelt, writer and President of the United States

It's time to have **Bold** faith.

Every tomorrow has two handles.
We can take hold of it with the handle of anxiety
or the handle of faith.
-Henry Ward Beecher,
clergy and abolitionist

Hope is putting faith to work when doubting
would be easier.
-Thomas S. Monson, President
Church of Jesus Christ of Latter-day Saints

Faith is deliberate confidence in the character of
God whose ways you may not understand at the
time.
-Oswald Chambers, evangelist

Doubt sees the obstacles.
Faith sees the way.
Doubt sees the darkest night.
Faith sees the day.
Doubt dreads to take a step
Faith soars high
Doubt questions
"Who believes?"
Faith answers "I."

Sometimes the best thing that you can do
is not to think,
not wonder,
not imagine,
not obsess.
Just breathe,
and have faith
that everything will work out for the best.

Faith is the bridge between where I am and where I want to be.

Pray as though everything depended on God. Work as though everything depended on you.
-Saint Augustine, theologian

Feed your faith, and your fears will starve to death.

Faith makes all things possible, but not
necessarily easy.

Faith consists in believing when it is beyond the
power of reason to believe.
- Voltaire, writer and activist

Good things will happen if you have faith and
believe with all your heart. It may take time, but
it will happen.

As your faith is strengthened you will find that
this no longer a sense of control,
that things will flow as they will,
and that you will flow with them,
to your great delight and benefit.
- Emmanuel Teney, physician and
Holocaust survivor

Smile when you're hurt.
Laugh when you want to cry.
Have faith in yourself when
nothing seems right.
Believe in your heart.
Trust that even though it is hard now,
in the end you'll be okay.

There will come a time when you believe
everything is finished. Have faith that that will
be the beginning.

Faithless is he that says farewell when the road
darkens.
- J.R.R. Tolkien, writer

Fear occupies the same space as Faith. And
there's only room for one.

Faith doesn't make sense that why it makes miracles

I have not lost faith in God. I have moments of anger and protest. Sometimes I've been closer to him for that reason.
-Elie Wiesel, writer and activist

Have faith, and follow through.

Keep trying.
Keep believing.
Be happy.
Don't get discouraged.
Things will work out.
- Gordon B. Hinckley, religious leader

Being great starts by
being fearless.
Fearless starts by
having faith.
Having faith starts by
letting go.
It's hard, but not impossible.

Faith means belief in something concerning
which doubt is theoretically possible.
- William James, philosopher

Sometimes life hits you in the head with a brick,
but don't lose faith.

I gave in, and admitted that God was God.
-C.S. Lewis, writer

Faith gives you an inner strength and a sense of
balance and perspective in life.

Now, God be praised, that to believing souls
gives light in darkness, comfort in despair.
-William Shakespeare, writer

More faith.
Less fear.

Believe in yourself.
Have faith in your abilities.
Without a humble but reasonable confidence
in your own powers
you cannot be successful or happy.
- Norman Vincent Peale, minister

No matter how far you have traveled,
or the failures that have gathered,
Hope would still meet you
anywhere.
- Dodinsky, writer

Take pride in how far you have come, and have faith in how far you can go!

We are never defeated unless we give up on God.
-Ronald Regan, President of the United States

Faith is the only thing I know that is stronger than fear!

Seasons of waiting are designed to prepare you, stretch your faith and get you ready for what comes next.

Faith is a knowledge within the heart, beyond the reach of proof.
- Khalil Gibran, poet

What would you attempt to do if you knew you could not fail?

For with faith to believe
what our eyes cannot see,
hope to look forward
to new joys to be,
and love to transform the
most commonplace
into beauty and kindness, and
goodness and grace. . .
for there is nothing too much to accomplish or
do . . . for faith, hope, and love
will carry us through

Faith is not about
everything turning out okay.
Faith is about being okay
no matter how things turn out.

True faith is doing what no one else is doing,
and traveling the road no one else travels.

A man of courage is also full of faith.
- Marcus Tullius Cicero, philosopher

When you have faith in yourself, you don't need
others to believe in you.

Faith is not belief without proof, but trust
without reservation.
- D. Elton Trueblood,
author and theologian

Don't lose hope. You never know what
tomorrow may bring.

The faith that stands on authority is not faith.
-Ralph Waldo Emerson, poet

Hope is wishing
something would happen.
Faith is believing
something will happen.
Courage is making
something happen.

A man can live about forty days
without food,
about three days
without water,
about eight minutes
without air,
but only for one second
without hope.
-Hal Lindsey, evangelist

Don't lose hope, the fog will lift.

Faith is a passionate intuition.
-William Wordsworth, poet

Hope shines brightest in the darkest moments.
Never give up!

Once you choose hope, anything is possible.

Faith has to do with things that are not seen and
hope with things that are not at hand.
- Thomas Aquinas, priest and philosopher

Faith is daring the soul to go beyond what the
eyes can see.

44 | P a g e

Most of the important things
in the world
have been accomplished
by people
who have kept on trying
when there seemed to be no hope at all.
- Dale Carnegie, motivational speaker

When people say you can't do it
– that it's impossible –
never lose hope.
Just because they couldn't
doesn't mean you can't.
-David Copperfield, illusionist

Believe in yourself and all that you are. Know
that there is something inside of you that is
greater than any obstacle.
-Christian D. Larson, author

God will make a way where there is no way!
-Philippians 2:13

Have faith in God; God has faith in you.
-Edwin Louis Cole, pastor

Life has two rules:
Rule 1 – Always have faith
Rule 2 – Always remember rule #1

To one who has faith, no explanation is
necessary. To one without faith, no explanation
is possible.
-Thomas Aquinas, priest and philosopher

Faith makes all things possible.
Love makes them easy.

Hold
On
Pain
Ends

Your mind is like a garden.
Your thoughts are the seeds.
The seeds of faith can grow flowers.
The seeds of doubt grow only weeds.

If you want to see the sunshine, you have to
have faith to weather the storm.

Faith and doubt both are needed – not as
antagonists, but working side by side to take us
around the unknown curve.
- Lillian Smith, author

Worry does not take way tomorrow's troubles, it
takes away today's peace. Have faith!

Faith means that you have peace even when you don't have all the answers.

Faith in oneself is the best and safest course.
-Michelangelo, artist

You may abandon hope. Hope never abandons you!

He who has faith has . . .
an inward reservoir of
courage,
hope,
confidence,
calmness, and
assuring trust that all will come out well
– even though to the world it may appear to
come out most badly.
- B.C. Forbes, journalist

The only faith that wears well and
holds its color
in all weathers
is that which is
woven of conviction and
set with the sharp mordant of experience.
- James Russell Lowell, poet

Doubt is not the opposite of faith; it is one
element of faith.
- Paul Tillich, philosopher

Believe in what you want and need. Fear is not
real.

To dream is to starve doubt and feed hope.
- Justina Chen Headley, writer

Worry only gives small things big shadows.
Have faith!

To me faith means not worrying.
- John Dewey, philosopher

Every weakness you have is a chance for God to
show his strength in your life. Have faith!

Hope is not a dream,
but a way of making
dreams become reality.
- L.J. Suenens, Cardinal

When you get into a tight place and
everything goes against you,
till it seems as though you
could not hang on a minute longer,
never give up then,
for that is just the place and time
that the tide will turn.
-Harriet Beecher Stowe, author

Always remember why there are storms.

Keep the faith, don't lose your perseverance and
always trust your gut instinct.
-Paula Abdul, entertainer

Follow your dreams. They know the way!

Don't ask how, ask what and why. Have faith, and let how worry about itself.

Faith, to my mind, is a stiffening process, a sort of mental starch.
-E.M. Forster, writer

Worry is a misuse of your imagination. Have faith!

The intellect has little to do
on the road to discovery.
There comes a leap in consciousness,
call it intuition or what you will,
and the solution comes to you and
you don't know how or why.
-Albert Einstein, physicist

As we allow the process of reinvention,
we often have to leave
jobs, locations, people, and things behind.
If it's true that we have a desire to rise to the
level of our highest potential, we need to truly
listen to our essential self.
It's the quiet voice, that asks us to up-level our
lives, be happier and more fulfilled, and it often
means we need to clear our elevator.
We have to draw boundaries around those
people and places that make us feel shackled.
This takes courage.
-Bethany Eaton, writer

Knowledge is only one half. Faith is the other.
- Novalis, author

Believe that you were given the life you were given because you are strong enough to lead it.

Keep your faith in God,
but keep your powder dry.
- Oliver Cromwell, military and political leader

The power of faith will often shine forth the most when the character is naturally weak.
- Augustus Hare, writer

I will have faith, and let go of all thoughts that do not make me strong.

Pray, and let God worry.
-Martin Luther, religious reformer

Next time you are stressed:
take a step back,
inhale and laugh.
Remember who you are,
and why you are here.
Have faith that you are never given
anything in this world
that you can't handle.
Be strong.
Be flexible.
Love yourself.
Love others.
Always remember,
just keep moving forward.

Each spring,
millions of flowers open
without anyone forcing the bud.
It reminds us to have faith and
not to force anything,
for things happen
at the right time.

Worry is spiritual short sight. Its cure is
intelligent faith.
- Paul Brunton, philosopher

Faith focuses on possibilities, not on problems.

Faith is the very first thing you should pack in a
hope chest.
-Sarah Ban Brethnach, writer

My reason nourishes my faith, and my faith my
reason.
- Norman Cousins, journalist

Have faith that you may not always end up
where you thought you would be, but you will
always end-up where you are supposed to be.

Reason is our soul's left hand,
faith her right.
- John Donne, poet

Imagine
with all your mind.
Believe
with all your heart.
Achieve
with all your might

You are braver
than you believe,
stronger
than you seem,
and smarter
than you think.
-A.A. Milne, writer

Be faithful in small things because it is in them
that your strength lies.
-Mother Teresa, humanitarian

Most important things in life are accomplished
when there seemed to be no more hope.

I hold that religion and faith are two different
things.
- Pat Buckley, philanthropist

It takes vision and courage to create, it takes
faith and courage to prove.
- Mason Cooley, aphorist

Standup to your fears. They don't have half of
the strength your faith does!

Faith is not something to grasp, it is a state to
grow into.
-Mahatma Gandhi, political activist

You gain strength, courage, and confidence
by every experience in which
you really stop to look fear in the face.
You are able to say to yourself,
"I lived through this horror.
I can take the next thing that comes along.
-Eleanor Roosevelt, political activist and
Former First Lady

Man, I just feel blessed . . .
I was in a situation where the only way I could
come out of it was by putting my faith in God.
No matter how good my lawyers were,
no matter how much celebrity I had,
everything was just stacked up against me.
-Sean Combs, entertainer

Faith is reason grown courageous.
- Sherwood Eddy, missionary and author

Hope is that little voice you hear whispering
"maybe" when it seems the entire world is
shouting "no."

Faith is not a thing which one 'loses,' we merely
cease to shape our lives by it.
- Georges Bernanos, author

I have learned that faith means trusting in advance what will only make sense in reverse.
- Philip Yancey, author

All the world is made of faith, and trust, and pixie dust.

The foundation stones for a balanced success are honest, character, integrity, faith, love and loyalty.
- Zig Ziglar, motivational speaker

No matter how dark things
seem to be or actually are,
raise your sights and see the possibilities
– always see them,
for they are always there.
-Norman Vincent Peale, author

One of the things I learned
the hard way was
that it doesn't pay to get discouraged.
Keeping busy and making optimism
a way of life can
restore your faith in yourself.
-Lucille Ball, actress

The reason birds can fly and we can't is simply because they have perfect faith, for to have faith is to have wings.
- J.M. Barrie, dramatist

Faith in God, includes faith in his timing.

Faith is being sure of what we hope for, and certain of what we do not see.
-Hebrews 11:1

Faith sees the invisible, believes the unbelievable, and receives the impossible.
- Corrie Ten Boom, author

When the world says, "Give up,"
Hope whispers, "Try it one more time."

At the point where hope would otherwise become hopelessness, it becomes faith.
- Robert Brault, operatic tenor

The human body has an enormous capacity for
adjusting to trying circumstances.
I have found that one can bear the unbearable
if one can keep one's spirits strong
even when one's body is being tested.
Strong convictions are the secret
of surviving deprivation;
your spirit can be full
even when your stomach is empty.
-Nelson Mandela, human rights activist and
South African President

I hope you never lose your sense of wonder,
You get your fill to eat but always keep that
hunger,
May you never take one single breath for
granted,
GOD forbid love ever leave you empty handed,
I hope you still feel small
when you stand beside the ocean,
Whenever one door closes I hope one more
opens,
Promise me that you'll give faith a fighting
chance,
And when you get the choice to sit it out or
dance.
-Lee Ann Womack, singer
I Hope You Dance

Don't look back in regret, but move on with hope and faith.

A small body of determined spirits fired by an unquenchable faith in their mission can alter the course of history.
-Mahatma Gandhi, political activist

Faith makes all things possible . . . love and passion make it worthwhile!

My faith helps me overcome such negative
emotions, and find my equilibrium.
- Dalai Lama, religious leader

Faith is sometimes all that you have when you
have nothing else.
If you still have faith, you have everything.

It's lack of faith that makes people afraid of
meeting challenges, and I believed in myself.
-Muhammad Ali, boxer

To get up
when you are down.
To fight more intensely
when you are intensely struggling.
To put in the extra effort
when you are in sheer pain.
To come back
when no one expects you to.
To have faith
when their seems to be no hope.
And to stand tall
when everyone is trying to pull you down
are what makes a champion.

Hope knows no fear.
Hope dares to blossom
even inside the abysmal abyss
Hope secretly feeds
and strengthens promises.
Hope and faith are two intimate brothers;
They always go together.
Hope nourishes faith and faith treasures hope.
- Sri Chinmoy, Indian spiritual master

Have the courage and faith to follow your heart
& intuition, they somehow already know what
you truly want to become.
- Steve Jobs, entrepreneur

Stand in faith. Even on your hard days.

What lies behind you and what lies in front of
you, is nothing compared to what lies within
you.
-Ralph Waldo Emerson, poet

Hope is faith holding out it's hand in the dark.
- George Iles, author

Have faith and stand for what you believe in,
even if that means standing alone.

Faith and prayer are the vitamins of the soul;
man cannot live in health without them.
- Mahalia Jackson, gospel singer

One of the things I learned the hard way
was that it doesn't pay to get discouraged.
Keeping busy and making optimism a way of life
can restore your faith in yourself.
-Lucille Ball, actress

I have learned over the years
that when one's mind is made up
this diminishes fear;
knowing what must be done
does away with fear.
-Rosa Parks, civil rights activist

Learn from yesterday, live for today, and hope for tomorrow.
-Albert Einstein, physicist

Have faith, and saddle-up anyway.

Every moment in life is an act of faith.
-Paulo Coelho, author

Don't fear change. Have faith that even though you may lose something good you will get given something better.

Hope is the one thing left to us in a bad time.
-E.B. White, writer

When fear knocks on the door, send faith and courage to meet it.

Hope
Sees the invisible
Feels the intangible
Conquers the impossible

Look back,
and thank God.
Look forward,
and trust God.
He closes doors no man can open,
and opens doors no man can close.

Truly, it is in the darkness that one finds the light, so when we are in sorrow, then this light is nearest of all to us.
-Meister Eckhart, philosopher

Stop being afraid of what could go wrong, and start having faith about what could go right.

Be willing to relinquish the life you've planned, so as to have the life that is waiting for you.
-Joseph Campbell, writer

Believe you can and you're halfway there.
-Theodore Roosevelt, explorer and
President of the United States

Faith is daring the soul to go beyond what the
eyes can see.

Believe in your dreams. They were given to you
for a reason.
- Katrina Mayer, author

I am like the grass.
I will come back greener and stronger.
I am the butterfly.
I will be stronger and more beautiful.
Every set back has within it the seeds of the
comeback. Healing takes faith and courage.
We all love faith and courage
even when we have to dig deep to find them.

But those who hope in the Lord
will renew their strength.
They will soar on wings like eagles.
They will run and not grow weary.
They will walk and not be faint.
-Isaiah 40:31

Sometimes your only transportation is a leap of faith.
- Margaret Shepherd, calligrapher

Stop trying to breathe life into the past. It died for a reason. Have faith. Let go, and move forward.

Life can only be understood backwards, but it must be lived forwards.
-Kierkegaard, philosopher

These are the times that try men's souls.
The summer soldier and the sunshine patriot
will,
in this crisis, shrink from
the service of their country;
but he that stands it now,
deserves the love and thanks
of men and women.
Tyranny, like hell,
is not easily conquered;
yet we have this consolation with us,
that the harder the conflict,
the more glorious the triumph.

What we obtain too cheap,
we esteem too lightly;
it is dearness only that
gives everything its value.
I love the man that can simile in trouble,
that can gather strength from distress
and grow brave by reflection.
'Tis the business of the little minds to shrink;
but he whose heart is firm,
and whose conscience approves his conduct,
will pursue his principles
unto death.
-Thomas Paine, patriot

The future comes one day at a time.
- Dean Acheson, statesman

God has perfect timing. He is never early and never late. It takes a little patience, and a lot of faith.

The future you shall know when it has come, before then forget it.
- Aeschylus, ancient Greek tragedian

So, so you made a lot of mistakes
Walked down the road a little sideways
Cracked a brick when you hit the wall
Yeah, you've had a pocketful of regrets
Pull you down faster than a sunset
Hey, it happens to us all
When the cold, hard rain just won't quit
And you can't see your way out of it
You find your faith that's been lost and shaken
You take back what's been taken
Get on your knees and dig down deep
You can do what you think is impossible
Keep on believing, don't give in
It'll come and make you whole again
It always will, it always does
Love is unstoppable
-Rascal Flatts, country music artists
Unstoppable

Go confidently in the direction of your dreams!
Live the life you have imagined.
As you simplify your life,
the laws of the universe will be simpler.
-Henry David Thoreau, writer

Doubt creates the mountains. Faith can move them.

The strongest man is the world is the one who can stand alone.
-Henrik Ibsen, writer

My faith is far bigger than my fear!

The world is full of magical things patiently
waiting for our sites to grow sharper.
- Bertrand Russell, philosopher

Faith is like sunlight, sometimes you have to rise
above the clouds to find it.

When you believe in something, believe in it all
the way, implicitly and unquestionably.
-Walt Disney, entertainment innovator

If I regarded my life from the point of view of
the pessimist, I should be undone.
I should seek in vain for the light that does not
visit my eyes and the music that does not ring in
my ears.
I should beg night and day and never be
satisfied.
I should sit apart in awful solitude,
a prey to fear and despair.
But since I consider it a duty to myself
and to others to be happy,
I escape a misery worse than
any physical deprivation.
-Helen Keller, writer and activist.

Faith teaches us to believe -
Faith teaches us to believe
that no matter what the situation is –
God has it.

To me faith means not worrying.
-John Dewey, philosopher

Live in the light created by faith.

Fear not for the future, weep not for the past.
-Percy Byssbe Shelley, poet

Dream with faith. Don't run from fears.

Faith includes noticing the mess, the emptiness
and discomfort, and letting it be there until
some light returns.
-Anne Lamott, writer

Faith is not the belief that God will do what you
want. It is the belief that God will do what is
right.

You do not need to know precisely what is
happening, or exactly where it is all going.
What you need is to recognize the possibilities
and
challenges offered by the present moment, and
to embrace them with
courage, faith and hope.
-Thomas Merton, writer

It is not the strongest
of the species that survives,
nor the most intelligent
that survives.
It is the one that is
the most adaptable to change.
-Charles Darwin, naturalist

You don't become what you want, you become
what you believe.
-Oprah Winfrey, entertainment mogul

Faith and a strong positive attitude will create
more miracles than any wonder drug.

If you think you can win, you can.
Faith is necessary to victory.
- William Hazlitt, essayist

Faith is the art of holding on to things your reason once accepted, despite your changing moods.
-C.S. Lewis, writer

Faith is not believing God can. It is knowing that he will.

Faith expects from God what is beyond all expectation.
- Andrew Murray, pastor and writer

As long as there is one upright man,
as long as there is one compassionate woman,
the contagion may spread and
the scene is not desolate.
Hope is the one thing left
to us in a bad time.
E.B. White, writer

When I despair,
I remember that all through history
the way of truth and love has always won.
There have been tyrants and murderers
and for a time they seem invincible,
but in the end,
they always fall . . .
think of it, always.
-Mahatma Gandhi, spiritual and political leader

If God shuts a door, stop banging on it. Have faith that whatever is behind it is not meant for you!

Faith is a living, daring confidence in God's grace, so sure and certain that a man could stake his life on it a thousand times.
-Martin Luther, religious reformer

Fear came knocking on the door. He heard the laughter within and promptly left!

The person who makes a success of living is the one who see his goal steadily and aims for it unswervingly.
-Cecil B. DeMille, film director

Faith says, "Quitting is not an option."

The obstacle is the path.
-Zen aphorism

Faith is walking face-first and full-speed into the
dark.
If we truly knew all the answers in advance
as to the meaning of life and the nature of God
and the destiny of our souls,
our belief would not be a leap of faith and
it would not be a courageous act of humanity;
it would just be... a prudent insurance policy.
-Elizabeth Gilbert, writer

In the happy moments,
praise God.
In the difficult moments,
seek God.
In the quiet moments,
have faith in God.
In every moment,
thank God.

You can do very little with faith, but you can do nothing without it.
- Samuel Butler, author

Faith is believing even when everything looks so wrong.

The future belongs to those who believe in the beauty of their dreams.
-Eleanor Roosevelt, political activist and Former First Lady

Things turn out best for the people who make
the best of the way things turn out.
- John R. Wooden, basketball player

It always seems impossible until it is done.

In faith there is enough light for those who want
to believe and enough shadows to blind those
who don't.
- Blaise Pascal, mathematician

The bravest are surely those who
have the clearest vision of
what is before them,
glory and danger alike, and
yet notwithstanding go out to meet it.
- Thucydides, Greek historian

None of us knows what might happen
even the next minute,
yet still we go forward. Because we trust.
Because we have Faith.
-Paulo Coelho, author
Brida

Nothing is built on stone, all is built on sand,
but we must build as if the sand were stone.
- Jorge Luis Borges, essayist

You must not be afraid to dream a little bigger.

We are wiser than we know.
-Ralph Waldo Emerson, author and poet

Faith is the bird that feels the light when the dawn is still dark.
- Rabindranath Tagore, author

There is no force equal to that of a determined person with faith.

All human wisdom is summed up in two words – wait and hope.
-Alexandre Dumas, writer

Courage and cheerfulness
will not only carry you over the rough places in
life,
but will enable you to bring comfort and help
to the weak-hearted and
will console you in the sad hours.
-William Osler, physician

On particularly rough days
when I am sure that I can't possibly endure,
I like to remind myself that
my track record for getting through
bad days so far is 100%,
and that's pretty good.
Have faith and carry on!

Faith is like radar that sees through the fog.
-Corrie Ten Boom, writer

You are a warrior. Warriors don't give up, or back down. They have faith and pick-up their sword and shield and fight.

Better to light a candle than to curse the darkness.
-Chinese proverb

Do not anticipate trouble, or worry about what may never happen. Keep in the sunlight.
-Benjamin Franklin, statesman

Giving up on a goal because of a setback is like slashing the other 3 tires because you got a flat. Have faith!

Pessimism never won any battle.
-Dwight D. Eisenhower, U.S. General and President

Trouble knocked on the door,
but hearing laughter
hurried away.
-Benjamin Franklin, statesman

A warrior feeds his body well
He trains it
Works on it
Where he lacks knowledge, he studies
But above all he must believe
He must believe in his strength
of will
of purpose
of heart and soul
- David Gemmell, author

I have had dreams and I have had nightmares, but I have conquered my nightmares because of my dreams.
- Jonas Salk, medical researcher

The temptation to quit will be greatest just before you are about to succeed. Have faith and go the distance.

To gain that which is worth having, it may be necessary to lose everything else.
-Bernadette Devlin, Politician and Activist

They can do all because they think they can.
-Virgil, philosopher

Have faith that everything is going to be all right. Maybe not today, but eventually.

Kid, you'll move mountains.
-Dr. Seuss, writer

The easiest thing to do
is to give up.
But to have faith and hold it together
when everyone else would understand
if you feel apart,
now that's true strength.

I believe in the sun
even when it is not shining.
I believe in love
even when I am alone.
I believe in God
even when he is silent.

You have to believe in yourself.
- Sun Tzu, philosopher and military general

Focus on what you can do, not on what you can't. Have faith and the small steps turn into miles.

We are who we believe we are.
-C.S. Lewis, writer

No matter how dark the moment, love & hope are always possible.
- George Chakiris, actor

God has you in the palm of his hand. He has never once failed before, and the good news is he is not about to start now.

The dry seasons in life do not last. The spring rains will come again.
-Sarah Ban Breathnach, writer

Never give in,
never give in,
never, never, never, never,
in nothing,
great or small,
large or petty.
Never give in except to
convictions of honor and good sense.
-Winston Churchill, British Prime Minister

There are two basic motivating forces:
fear and love.
When we are afraid, we pull back from life.
When we are in love, we open to all that life has
to offer with passion, excitement, and
acceptance.
We need to learn to love ourselves first,
in all our glory and our imperfections.
If we cannot love ourselves,
we cannot fully open to our ability
to love others or our potential to create.
Evolution and all hopes for a better world
rest in the fearlessness and open-hearted
vision of people who embrace life.
-John Lennon, musician

Plunge into the deep without fear, with the
gladness of April in your heart.
-Rabindranath Tagore, writer

No matter how you feel, get up, dress up, and
show up. Have faith and never give up.

It's not whether you get knocked down, it's
whether you get up.
-Vince Lombardi, football coach

Fear is only as deep as the mind allows.
-Japanese proverb

Have faith that God didn't bring you this far to
a abandon you.

Strength comes from waiting.
-Jose Marti, writer

Any road followed precisely to its end
leads precisely nowhere.
Climb the mount just a little bit
to test it is a mountain.
From the top of the mountain,
you cannot see the mountain.
-Frank Herbert, writer

Sometimes I thank God
for unanswered prayers
Remember when you're talkin'
to the man upstairs
That just because he may not answer
doesn't mean he don't care
Some of God's greatest gifts
are unanswered prayers
-Garth Brooks, country music great
Unanswered Prayers

Dream! Dream! And then go for it!
-Desmond Tutu, activist

Sometimes good things fall apart so that better things can fall together. Have faith that they will fall together.

Truly, it is in darkness that one finds the light, so when we are in sorrow, then this light is nearest of all to us.
-Meister Eckhart, mystic

What is harder than rock, or softer than water?
Yet soft water hollows out hard rock. Persevere.
- Ovid, poet

Have faith that God is in control even when
everything seems out of control.

All of our dreams can come true if we have the
courage to pursue them.
-Walt Disney, entertainment entrepreneur

Often the difference between
a successful person and a failure
is not one's better abilities or ideas,
but the faith that one has in one's ideas,
to take a calculated risk and
go forward.

Forget past mistakes.
Forget failures.
Forget everything except
what you're going to do now
and do it.
-Will Durant, historian

Imagination will often carry us to worlds that never were. But without it we go nowhere.
- Carl Sagan, astronomer

Have faith that you have what it takes, but it is going to take everything you have got.

Faith is believing in something when common sense tells you not to.
-Miracle on 34th Street

Turn your face to the sun and the shadows fall
behind you.
-Maori proverb

Maybe it's not always about trying to fix
something that is broken. Maybe it's about
having the faith to start over and creating
something better.

Whether you think you can or whether you
think you can't, you're right.
-Henry Ford, industrialist

When you have faith,
you can look fear straight
in the eyes and say,
"Get the hell out of my way.
I have things to do."

Commit yourself to a dream . . .
Nobody who tries to do something great but
fails is a total failure. Why? Because he can
always rest assured that he succeeded in life's
most important battle – he defeated the fear of
trying.
-Robert H Schuller, pastor

The worse a situation becomes, the less it takes
to turn it around, and the bigger the upside.
-George Soros, financier

True faith is a perfect compass.

The only real prison is fear, and the only real
freedom is freedom from fear.
-Aung San Suu Kyi, political activist

We must embrace the pain and burn it as fuel
for our journey.
-Kenji Miyazawa, writer

If you don't fit in, have faith that you are
probably doing the right thing.

Some people think that as soon as you plant a
tree, it must bear fruit. We must allow it grow a
bit.
-Tunku Abdul Rahman Putra, politician

Have faith and never regret anything
that has happened in your life.
It happened for a reason.
It cannot be changed, undone or totally
forgotten.
So take it is as a lesson learned,
and move on.

I am not who I ought to be.
I know I'm not all that I want to be.
But I've come a long way
from who I used to be.
I have faith that I won't give up
on becoming what I am supposed to be.

Life brings tears, smiles, and memories. Have faith that the tears dry, the smiles fade, but the memories last forever.

Nothing will ever be attempted if all possible objections must first be overcome.
-Samuel Jackson, actor

It's not about being the best. It's about having faith that you are better than you were yesterday.

A hunch is creativity trying to tell you
something.
-Frank Capra, film director

The moment you feel like giving up, have faith
and remember all the reasons you held on for so
long.

Know from whence you came. If you know
from whence you came, there are absolutely no
limitations on where you can go.
-James Baldwin, writer

Some chapters are sad.
Some chapters are happy.
Some chapters are exciting.
But if you don't have the faith
to turn the page,
you will never know
what the next chapter holds.

Life is too short to wake up
in the morning with regrets.
So, love the people who treat you right, and
forget about the ones who don't.
Have faith that everything happens for a reason.
If you get a chance, take it.
If it changes your life, let it.
Nobody said that it would be easy.
They promised you it would be worth it.

My hopes are not always realized, but I always hope.
-Ovid, poet

Don't dwell on what went wrong. Instead, have faith and focus on what to do next. Spend your energies on moving forward to find the answer.

We don't see things as they are, we see them as we are.
- Anais Nin, author

Be strong, because things will get better. It may be stormy now, but have faith it never rains forever.

A baby is God's opinion that life should go on.
-Carl Sandburg, writer and editor

Have faith and let go of the thoughts that do not make you strong.

I think if I've learned anything about friendship,
it's to hang in, stay connected, fight for them,
and let them fight for you.
Don't walk away, don't be distracted,
don't be too busy or tired,
don't take them for granted.
Friends are part of the glue that holds
life and faith together.
Powerful stuff.
-Jon Katz, writer

Good things come to those
who believe.
Better things come to those
who are patient.
The best things come to those
who have faith and don't give up.

Don't lose faith. When the sun goes down, the stars come out.

Don't worry about the darkness, turn on the light. The darkness automatically goes away.
-David Lynch, film director

The reason most people give up is because they lack faith. They look at how far they still have to go, instead of how far they have come.

Be strong enough to let go, and patient enough
to wait with faith for what you deserve.

We can easily forgive a child who is afraid of the
dark. The tragedy of life is when men are afraid
of the light.
-Plato, philosopher and teacher

Have faith that you are far too smart to be the
only thing standing in your way.

Dear God,
If today I lose my hope
remind me
that your plans
are better than my dreams

Always remember that your present situation
is not your final destination.
Faith is future focused.
The best is yet to come.

If you put off everything until you are absolutely sure, you will never get anything done.
-Norman Vincent Peele, writer

Have faith that God will wreck your plans when he sees that your plans are about to wreck you.

If you set goals and go after them with all the faith and determination you can muster, your gifts will take you places that will amaze you.
-Les Brown, composer

Have faith and start living your life fearlessly.

Do not go where the path may lead, go instead where there is no path and leave a trail.
-Ralph Waldo Emerson, writer and poet

That voice in your head that says "you can't do this" is a liar.

Surround yourself with
the dreamers,
the doers,
the believers, and
the thinkers,
but most of all surround yourself with
those who have faith and
see the greatness in you.

Someday, we will forget the hurt,
the reason we cried, and
who caused us pain.
We will finally realize that
the secret of being free is not revenge,
but having faith and letting things unfold
in their own way and time.
After all, what matters is not the first,
but the last chapter of our life
which shows how well we ran the race.
So smile, laugh, forgive, have faith and
love all over again.

If you get a chance, take it, if it changes your life, have faith and let it.

There are two ways to live. You can live as if nothing is a miracle, or you can live as if everything is a miracle.
-Albert Einstein, physicist

We can't always see where the road leads, but God promises there's something better up ahead we just have to have faith and trust him.

Those who don't believe in magic will never find it.
-Ronald Dahl, novelist

Dreams come in sizes too big so that we can grow into them.

There is no passion to be found in settling for a life that is less than the one you are capable of living.
-Nelson Mandela, political leader

Have faith
that God did not add another day to your life
because you needed it.
He added it
because someone out there
needed you.

Once we believe
we can risk
curiosity,
wonder,
spontaneous delight or
any experience that
reveals the human spirit.
-E.E. Cummings, writer

Doubt your doubts before you doubt your faith.
- Dieter F. Uchtdorf, aviator

Have faith and strength will find you even
sooner than you thought it would.

You are never too old to set another goal or
dream a new dream.
-C.S. Lewis, writer

Follow your personal legend and the universe
will conspire to give you what you need.
-Paulo Coelho, writer

All hope is born in the dark.

Your future is as bright as your faith.
-Thomas S. Monson, President of
The Church of the Latter-day Saints

If an egg is broken by an outside force,
life ends.
If an egg is broken by an inside force,
life begins.
Have faith that great things
always begin from inside.

Have faith.
Whatever comes.
Let it come.
Whatever stays.
Let it stay.
Whatever goes.
Let it go!

Faith is spiritualized imagination.
- Henry Ward Beecher, pastor

Amazing people don't just happen. Have faith
amazing is what you were meant to be.

As I look back on my life, I realize that every
time I thought I was being rejected from
something good, I was actually being re-directed
to something better.
-Steve Maraboli, writer

One of the happiest moments
in life
is when you find
the faith and courage
to let go
of what
you can't change.

IN THE END,

ALWAYS CHOOSE FAITH!

Made in the USA
Columbia, SC
15 September 2022

67354213R00104